Songs of Nature

"This is a book of great luminosity. Light breaks out everywhere—in beauty, truth, and ultimately in the Divine Presence. The lens of the camera become the eyes of the soul penetrating both the beautiful and the brutal in human existence. The Psalms make clear that life always has potential for both. . . The author makes herself vulnerable to us, revealing a person who is deeply human. In doing so she probes us to look honestly into the core of our being. Her suggestion of personal journaling moves us toward a more courageous and meditative examination of who we are and what we are here for. For those who seek to move beyond the mundane to the spiritual, I strongly recommend Rebecca Webb Wilson as a wise and delightful companion on the journey."

Brooks Ramsey, Marriage and Family Therapist
Ordained Minister, The American Baptist Convention

"The ability to capture and share is the role of the blessed photographer. Becky Wilson's new book documents her point of view of the world she travels, and her photography inspires all of us and gives us the opportunity to wonder."

Jack Kenner, Photographer

"Becky Wilson has captured the beauty of creation with her camera and the beauty of the Psalms and her own thoughts to lead us into new beginnings as we consider our awesome God."

Katharine A. Phillips, Teaching Director
and Regional Conference Speaker, Community Bible Study

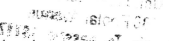

"Becky Wilson shares with us the images she has captured with her camera, and the meditations she has stored in her heart. In this book she invites us also to look at creation and the reflections of our lives, and through them to encounter the Living God of both. She encourages us to take time daily to look and reflect, and in the process to encounter God at a deeper level."

William Clemmons, Retired professor of Christian Spirituality

Songs of Nature
Meditations in Psalms

Rebecca Webb Wilson

PROVIDENCE HOUSE PUBLISHERS
Franklin, Tennessee

Printed in the United States of America

05   04   03   02   01   1   2   3   4   5

Library of Congress Catalog Card Number: 2001091672

ISBN: 1-57736-246-2

Cover design by Gary Bozeman and Elaine Kernea Wilson
Cover photo by Rebecca Webb Wilson

PROVIDENCE HOUSE PUBLISHERS
238 Seaboard Lane Franklin, Tennessee 37067
800-321-5692
www.providencehouse.com

To my dad, Donald Ross Webb Jr.,

and to the memory of my mother,

Rebecca Cobb Webb

PREFACE

Let the words of my mouth and the meditations of my heart
be acceptable in thy sight, O Lord, my strength and my Redeemer.—Psalm 19:1 KJV

Years ago my husband and I went to Ireland for a week with my parents. What a magical time we saw more rainbows than we imagined possible. We even pulled off the narrow, winding road to run in a stone-strewn emerald field where the rainbow ended, looking for the pot of gold. The real treasure I found was the time we had laughing and exploring with my parents, away from our collective responsibilities.

My parents have profoundly affected my outlook on life as they have loved and encouraged me in every endeavor. They never pushed me to follow their direction but prayed I would find my own. They gave me a King James Version of the Bible (that was about the only version available) on my twelfth birthday. Some years later, tucked away within its pages, I discovered in my mother's handwriting this promise: "Remember this—you will not face a decision or enter a door that a prayer has not preceded you." I believe their prayers have eased my way through life's difficulties.

This verse from Psalm 19 was my mother's favorite verse and shows the priorities she held. She carefully guarded her tongue from saying hurtful words and kept the word of God in front of her constantly. One of my clearest memories is of the nightly time together in my parents' bedroom. Mother, in her gown, stood at her dresser using it like a lectern or sat on the bed with her Bible in her lap, and read aloud the scripture for that day as outlined in our Baptist Training Union quarterly.

I pray that these words and meditations are acceptable to God and I dedicate them to my parents. They have incorporated the words and the spirit of the Bible into the fabric of their lives in such a way that they made it easy for my sister and me to seek God's strength and believe in the possibility of redemption. And that reminds me of rainbows.

ACKNOWLEDGMENTS

I wish to thank my children, Spence Lee Wilson Jr., Rebecca Wilson Macsovits, Lauren Wilson Young, and Webb Wilson for their unbelievable patience and restraint on countless family trips when my camera slowed them down to a snail's pace. I also wish to acknowledge my sister, Carmen Anderson, and my closest friend, Patricia Allen Lackey, for the many trips over the years they have endured with me and my Minolta and for even encouraging my vice as a profligate with film. For thirteen years my mother-in-law, Dorothy Lee (Mrs. Kemmons) Wilson, accompanied me and my sisters-in-law, Betty Wilson Moore, Carole Wilson West, Norma Thompson Wilson, and Susan Cooper Wilson on our "Wilson Women Trips" various scenic places where my camera seldom stopped clicking. To them and to her memory I acknowledge my immense gratitude. And of course, above all, I want to thank my husband, Spence Wilson, who has borne not only my eccentricities but also, on occasions, my camera equipment. Without his support and appreciation of my passion for beauty and travel, this dream would never have come true. I love you all.

INTRODUCTION

I make a fresh start in autumn, perhaps because the fall and the beginning of the school year always excited me as a child. There were new, intriguing books, boxes of rainbow-colored crayons, blank notebook paper, and the smell of new leather shoes. Perhaps it's the cooling air finally coming to the South that quickens my summer-baked body and nudges me from my sluggishness to begin to get things done again. Whatever its origins, this is my new year, not January first, complete with lists and resolutions and bold ideas.

So I wanted to create a journal that was not irrevocably tied to a particular date on which to begin. Spring may stir your creative juices, or your birthday, or another day of special significance. The primary thing is to begin when you feel so moved. You may take the time to meditate only once a week, but you may discover that you want to do it more frequently and cover more space than is allowed by these pages. Use the blank pages in the back or start a notebook for "overflow."

It is with much gratitude that I recognize the great privilege I have had to travel. My first airplane trip was at age sixteen when I flew halfway around the world to the Philippines as an American Field Service exchange student. After graduation from college, I was a flight attendant for Pan American World Airways and never got enough of seeing new faces and places.

As a wife, attorney, and mother of four, I have continued my love affair with the exotic. Having my camera in hand, trying to catch the perfect light or the perfect encounter with wildlife has provided me with some of my most satisfying days. Because I've been blessed to have my family or best friend along to share many of these moments, the pictures I take have also created a wonderful, invisible tapestry of memories which unfolds whenever I revisit them.

Perhaps some of these pictures will remind you of special times and places in your own life. It is my hope that in seeing this incredibly colorful, diverse, and beautiful world through these photographs, punctuated with verses from Psalms, you might have a personal revelation of the awe-inspiring power and love of our Creator. If possible, find a quiet place with few distractions in which to meditate. Turn off the phone. There are no set rules, no one right way to meditate.

Look at the picture and let your mind go. Does it call up any particular emotion? Jot that down. Read the scripture and the thought that goes with it. Think a bit about what you read and see. Write short phrases if you prefer them over complete sentences. [Note: In order to best reproduce the colors of the photographs, it was necessary to print this book on glossy paper. Not all pens work well on this finish—I recommend a fine-tip pen with quick-drying ink.]

By reading the verses each day, you may actually memorize them by the end of the week and will recall them by associating the passage with their illustrations. In this way, you will build a lasting spiritual resource. By slowing down a few minutes on a regular basis, you may find that God has a message for you. It begins with "I love you."

Songs of Nature

WEEK 1

Blessed is the man that walketh not in the counsel of the ungodly,
nor standeth in the way of sinners, nor sitteth in the seat of the scornful.
But his delight is in the law of the Lord; and in his law doth he meditate day and
night. And he shall be like a tree planted by the rivers of water,
that bringeth forth his fruit in his season; his leaf also shall not wither;
and whatsoever he doeth shall prosper.—Psalm 1:1–3 KJV

The first scripture I ever memorized, in the first grade, was the first Psalm. Thank you, Mrs. Weaver. It was indelibly imprinted on that fresh mind, eager to learn, more eager to please a kind lady. What a gift she gave us with that discipline. It was a valuable example of an adult, outside the home and church, who thought the Bible was very important. She taught us the rewards of memorization, which have lasted a lifetime, and the content of the verses, which has proven to be a short formula for real joy.

Like these now massive live oaks lovingly put in the ground as saplings by a plantation owner 150 years ago, we, too, are planted by God to grow strong and flourish wherever we are. We are watered by passing people: parents, pastors, friends, and sometimes even by strangers. Who has nurtured you in the past month? Whose soul have you watered this week?

JOURNAL THOUGHTS

_____

_____

_____

_____

_____

_____

_____

_____

_____

WEEK 2

O Lord my God, I take refuge in you;
save and deliver me from all who pursue me,
or they will tear me like a lion and rip me to pieces
with no one to rescue me.—Psalm 7:1

On a game drive in South Africa outside Kruger National Park we were tracking two male lions early ne morning. In the distance we saw a small herd of ildebeest grazing. To the right of our Land Rover, a oness materialized from the bush. She took in the tuation immediately and crept through the brush, eing the unknowing prey.

In a matter of minutes she sprang into the now anicked herd and seized one female by the throat to 1oke her to death. Two other lionesses joined her to take own the beast. After the wildebeest died, the two male ons we had been tracking arrived on the scene and staked their unearned but preeminent claim to the kill. They then proceeded to tear the huge animal apart and feast on it for several hours, without ever allowing the females to have a taste.

Whether it is past mistakes, competitors in the workplace, a hurtful relationship . . . there are times when you are frantically running from someone or something that seems overwhelming. You feel totally alone and vulnerable. You may feel like letting the lions do their thing just to get it over with. Do not despair. God can make a safe place for you to face your fears and will stand with you to do so.

JOURNAL THOUGHTS

_____

_____

_____

_____

_____

_____

_____

_____

WEEK 3

O Lord, our Lord, how majestic is your name in all the earth!
You have set your glory above the heavens . . .
When I consider your heavens the works of your fingers,
the moon and the stars which you have set in place,
what is man that you are mindful of him, the son of man that you care for him?
You made him a little lower than the heavenly beings
and crowned him with glory and honor.—Psalm 8:1, 3–5

It is our last night in Africa, on a wonderful safari that has taken us through northern Tanzania, Victoria Falls in Zimbabwe, and now the Okavanga Delta in Botswana. There have been many beautiful nights under myriad arrays of constellations. Some, like the Southern Cross, are new to us who grew up in the Northern Hemisphere. It is still, and as the full moon breaks through the darkening clouds, we see stately giraffes gliding dreamlike across the grassy veldt headed home for the night as we will head home tomorrow.

A black velvet sky pinned together with jeweled sta[rs] or glowing with a burnished moon evokes hushed awe [of] the magnificent Creator. It invites us to pause wi[th] wonder no matter where we are: whether we are gett[ing] into our car in a darkened parking lot, lying on a pallet [in] our back yard or pushing the trash can down the drivewa[y.] A free gift all of us can receive most nights, every mon[th] . . . if only we look up.

JOURNAL THOUGHTS

_____
_____
_____
_____
_____
_____
_____

WEEK 4

Show me the wonder of your great love,
you who save by your right hand those who take refuge in you from their foes.
Keep me as the apple of your eye;
hide me in the shadow of your wings.—Psalm 17:7–9

Years ago when I was practicing law in downtown Memphis, I began watching the red-tailed hawks perched in treetops and on electrical towers along the expressway. During the winter they could predictably be found, each in its own territory. They seemed to have staked out an area about one to two miles long. I began taking binoculars with me in the car and often pulled off on the shoulder of the busy highway to watch them soar and hunt.

Several people I worked with observed my behavior, and one finally suggested I get a bumper sticker that announced "I Brake for Hawks." From then on, I've had an affinity for hawks in general. I always feel my day is especially blessed when I sight one of these majestic birds and stand beneath its wings.

Hiding in the shadow of God's wing is a beautiful image. With most nesting birds, the eggs and then the fledglings are protected when most vulnerable by the outspread wings of the parents. When I am feeling particularly fragile and exposed to adversities, it is comforting to know that God still loves me and takes me under his wings.

JOURNAL THOUGHTS

_____

_____

_____

_____

_____

_____

_____

WEEK 5

It is God who arms me with strength
and makes my way perfect.
He makes my feet like the feet of a deer;
he enables me to stand on the heights.—Psalm 18:32–33

Deer seem so soft and fragile with their limpid, soulful eyes. Yet God has made them remarkably surefooted, enabling them to climb to heart-stopping elevations and to cross craggy terrain unapproachable for humans. What a view they must have once they've reached the heights! Do they see the world more from God's perspective there? When God leads us up the mountains of our lives, is it so we might see more, and farther, too?

I have lurched along, tripping over my own ego a staggering under the weight of my own arrogance more occasions than I care to admit. But there have be moments, with God's grace and direction, when my ste were swift and sure, and I made it to the mountain. T view is exhilarating . . . but it is impossible to stay there. I just hope to return again. Help me not to get the way of your plan, Lord.

JOURNAL THOUGHTS

_____

_____

_____

_____

_____

_____

_____

_____

_____

WEEK 6

God makes a huge dome for the sun—a superdome!
The morning sun's a new husband leaping from his honeymoon bed,
the day breaking sun an athlete racing to the tape.
That's how God's Word vaults across the skies from sunrise to sunset,
melting ice, scorching deserts, warming hearts to faith.
The revelation of God is whole and pulls our lives together.
The signposts of God are clear and point out the right road.
The life-maps of God are right, showing the way to joy.
—Psalm 19:4(b)–8 THE MESSAGE

For the past three years I've tried to run two or three days a week. I'm really a night person, but if I don't get up and run at 6:00 A.M., then I don't do it later. Too many other things interfere: errands take longer; the phone jangles more often; meetings have to be prepared for and attended. Then there's carpool, and suddenly it's time to cook dinner, and there is no time to run.

Consequently, because of this one change in habit, I've seen more sunrises in the last few years than in the rest of my life combined! I run with the sun and commune with God. It has become a time for me to sing songs of praise, to talk about concerns of family and friends, to focus on the world around me, and to let God speak to me. Paying attention to the signposts early in the day keeps me from getting lost later.

You might try a variation of this approach. Get up fifteen minutes earlier than you usually do and either go outside to walk or sit. Or take a chair by a window so you can look out to see the sun's early rays brighten the sky. Enjoy the peace of sharing your first moments of a new day with your Creator.

JOURNAL THOUGHTS

_____

_____

_____

_____

_____

_____

WEEK 7

But you, O Lord, be not far off;
O my Strength, come quickly to help me.
Deliver my life from the sword,
my precious life from the power of the dogs.
Rescue me from the mouth of the lions;
save me from the horns of the wild oxen.—Psalm 22:19–21

The first time I had a close look at wild dogs was in Tanzania and later, on the same trip, in South Africa. Their strange, tricolored patchwork is very distinctive and different from domestic dogs. But their playfulness and camaraderie within their pack reminds me of a large litter of regular puppies. However, make no mistake; as a group they are the most successful hunters of antelope in Africa.

Their power is amazing and is based not only on their speed, which can reach up to thirty-five miles per hour; but also on their endurance. They can run at that speed for at least two miles. Seeing these unusual creatures in their own habitat, and looking closely at their serrated teeth, designed to rip and tear efficiently, makes this very more vividly real.

We all have wild dogs in our lives that catch up with early in life and run with us through the years. We have trouble shaking them off our trail, and they can strike fe in our hearts as they gain on our heels. They may be deb that bite us and try to pull us down. They may jealousies that jump on our hearts. Whatever they are, matter how long they have been with you, God can deliv you from your own wild dogs. Ask the Lord to travel wi you and protect you.

JOURNAL THOUGHTS

_____

_____

_____

_____

_____

_____

WEEK 8

God, my shepherd! I don't need a thing.
You have bedded me down in lush meadows,
you find me quiet pools to drink from.
True to your word, you let me catch my breath
and send me in the right direction.—Psalm 23:1–3 THE MESSAGE

As much as I would like to blame God or someone else for the frenetic pace I keep, I can't. I drive myself to distraction: staying busy, meeting deadlines, checking off to-do lists. I am like the other sheep in our modern, urban world, running different directions, being pushed to excel and to be productive twenty-four hours a day, seven days a week. We tend to focus on the "Yea, though I walk through the valley of the shadow of death," part of this psalm, when actually we spend relatively little of our life span in that valley and most of it in the meadows getting there.

Perhaps I need to pay more attention to the ways of getting there. God shows us the quiet pools, but we have to decide to drink from them. There are many resting places which the Creator has made for us along our journey—spaces to renew our soul, our spirit, and our commitments. And we all have the same twenty-four-hour day and fifty-two-week year with which to work. May we have the wisdom to use them well.

JOURNAL THOUGHTS

WEEK 9

The earth is the Lord's and everything in it,
the world and all who live in it;
for he founded it upon the seas
and established it upon the waters.—Psalm 24:1–2

I am drawn to water: splashing in a stone fountain, foaming white in a raging river, lapping the shore of a mountain lake, or pounding a sandy beach. It can thrill or soothe or frighten. I read that 74 percent of the earth's surface is covered by water and that 65 percent of my own body is comprised of it. We cannot live much beyond three days without it. Scientists say that life itself began in the seas. The Bible and biology seem to agree. Our own births, preceded by a rush of life-giving waters which had nurtured and protected us, mirror that.

How exquisitely analogous are these births to t symbol of our spiritual birth: baptism with water. We d to old ways and rise out of the waters with new life, n direction. Then, too, Jesus told the Samaritan woman the well that he could give her living water, that is, beli in him would give her eternal life. But if these though are difficult to deal with initially, we are also admonish simply to give water to those who are thirsty, even to t least of our brothers and sisters, and by doing so, we a giving it to God.

JOURNAL THOUGHTS

_____

_____

_____

_____

_____

_____

_____

WEEK 10

One thing I ask of the Lord, this is what I seek
that I may dwell in the house of the Lord all the days of my life,
to gaze upon the beauty of the Lord and to seek him in his temple.
For in the day of trouble he will keep me safe in his dwelling;
he will hide me in the shelter of his tabernacle
and set me high upon a rock.—Psalm 27:4–5

arge rocks and boulders dominate the landscape in the Southwest. For many Indian tribes they provided a ling place from wild animals and from enemies. The asazi, a Navajo term for "ancient ones," built their ages or pueblos on the tops of high mesas as far back 750 A.D. as a means of protection from any passing rauders. In northeastern Arizona the Hopis today live First, Second, and Third Mesas.

I can picture us perched on the fortress of God's ck, raised above the frightening desert with its alien terrain, lack of water, and hungry predators. Daily we have to travel through strange territory, but we have a safe place to come to at the end of the day.

In a world of much uncertainty, superficial connections, and dwindling ethical leadership, God's unchanging love for us is a strong foundation on which to put our faith. Such a rock provides shade to refresh us from the heat of stress and a secure handhold when the turbulence of sudden storms tries to drown us.

JOURNAL THOUGHTS

_____

_____

_____

_____

_____

_____

_____

WEEK 11

The voice of the Lord is over the waters;
the voice of the Lord is powerful; the voice of the Lord is majestic . . .
The Lord sits enthroned over the flood; the Lord is enthroned as King forever.
The Lord gives strength to his people;
the Lord blesses his people with peace.—Psalm 29:3–4; 10–11

Thunder is one of God's voices that reminds us of his immense power as it rolls and rumbles like pins in a giant bowling alley tumbling across the sky. Cody, one of our big German shepherds who usually looks so fierce, is totally intimidated by the sounds of a storm coming. He once clawed through the screen on our den window trying to get inside and away from the noise.

God's voice sometimes frightens me, too, when I believe I'm being told to do something I don't want to or don't think I am capable of doing. The fear of bei foolish or failing takes hold. And I have run the oppos way, trying to escape the voice. I am learning, however, I listen and do what God leads me to do, he gets through it with a great sense of peace at being in his w I may even hear that still, small voice of God say, "W done, my good and faithful servant."

JOURNAL THOUGHTS

WEEK 12

Sing to the Lord, you saints of his; praise his holy name.
For his anger lasts only a moment, but his favor lasts a lifetime;
weeping may remain for a night, but rejoicing comes in the morning.
You turned my wailing into dancing; you removed my sackcloth and
clothed me with joy, that my heart may sing to you and not be silent.
O Lord my God, I will give you thanks forever.—Psalm 30:4–5; 11–12

These verses underscore the difference in God's time and our time—the possible subject for a second Theory of Relativity. We grow impatient when we pray and demand that change come immediately. Years on our calendar may pass before we see the real answer to a particular prayer. When we are in the midst of personal or family crises and think God has turned a deaf ear to us, the days drag endlessly on. These adversities are just a wink of an eye for the Deity and just a few seconds, relatively speaking, to the hours of blessings each individual receives over his or her life span.

What a promise! God loves us forever and even though we endure the loss of loved ones, physical hardships, and financial difficulties, sorrow does not have the last word. We can find joy again. When the flood destroyed Noah's world, the rainbow became a holy sign of God's covenant with mankind and all life on earth that he keeps his promises.

JOURNAL THOUGHTS

_____

_____

_____

_____

_____

_____

_____

WEEK 13

Let me give you some good advice;
I'm looking you in the eye and giving it to you straight:
"Don't be ornery like a horse or mule that needs bit and bridle to stay on track."
God defiers are always in trouble; God affirmers find themselves loved every time
they turn around. Celebrate God. Sing together—everyone!
All you honest hearts, raise the roof!—Psalm 32:8–10 THE MESSAGE

In recent summers we have visited close friends on a ranch in Montana for a few days for the fourth of July. We always ride several hours during our stay. Each time I go, I am given a rudimentary lesson because they realize it's my annual horseback outing, and I am not a natural rider. Even with a bit and bridle, those horses just know I'm out of my league and get a bit frisky. Without those essentials, I would lose all control.

I guess I don't like these verses because they speak so directly to me, as I have been called "mule-headed" more than once. It's one thing to be tenacious, but quite another to be so obstinate as to insist on doing everything your way, regardless. It is so easy to get into the habit of making quick decisions and becoming very proud of being so decisive. Often the better decision can be made based on consensus over a longer time frame. Trusting in God to direct us relieves us of a lot of the stress and pressure we generate when we try to do everything alone. It also lightens our hearts so we do feel like celebrating.

JOURNAL THOUGHTS

_____

_____

_____

_____

_____

_____

_____

WEEK 14

Both high and low among men find refuge in the shadow of your wings.
They feast on the abundance of your house;
you give them drink from your river of delights.
For with you is the fountain of life; in your light we see light.—Psalm 36:7–9

first met the Dorobo people in Ernest Hemingway's *Green Hills of Africa*. In the opening sentence, he ferred to the Wanderobo, as they were then called. Today ey are still hunter-gatherers in Tanzania, where they ve lived for centuries, little touched by the quantum anges that the rest of the world has experienced. Stone ge rhythms and patterns, rather than twentieth-century ssonance, orchestrate their lives.

For two days our family walked and hunted with three orobo men. They carry virtually all their possessions on eir bodies at all times. Each has three metal-tipped andmade arrows in his quiver, and the poison with which coat them so that when they strike big game, the imal will drop sooner rather than later. They also pack firestarter, a drinking reed (which lets them drink the eaner water in the bottom of pools), and a "magic stick" make themselves invisible to their prey. When asuccessful in their hunting, they seek out beehives high up in the giant baobab trees. After smoking out the bees, they feast on the wild honey.

These people have already mastered the art of bare essentials that we read about in *Living the Simple Life* and *Don't Sweat the Small Stuff*. Some consider them the lowest among humanity, and undoubtedly their lives are harsh. Yet, watching their enthusiasm and almost childlike delight in greeting the wonders of each new day teaches us a lot about priorities. They live at peace in true community, knowing that their mutual survival depends on it. They are free to go and come and follow the game trails without punching time clocks. They don't stress out about getting a promotion, buying the newest utility vehicle, or sending the children to the best private school. They think they are rich. How can we simplify our own daily routine so we, too, are freer to follow God's trail and see the wonders around us? What can you eliminate this week from your schedule in order to do this?

JOURNAL THOUGHTS

_____

_____

_____

_____

_____

WEEK 15

*The days of the blameless are known to the Lord,
and their inheritance will endure forever. In times of disaster they will not wither;
in days of famine they will enjoy plenty. But the wicked will perish:
the Lord's enemies will be like the beauty of the fields,
they will vanish—vanish like smoke.—Psalm 37:18–20*

I don't know the names of the small-minded people who called my grandfather a "nigger lover." Clearly, they had observed his kindness to field hands over the years in rural West Tennessee. Their names have vanished like the spent sunflowers will. I never met my mother's father because he died the year before I was born. To some extent, however, I do know him because of the warm memories my grandmother, my mother, and my aunts have shared with me.

In 1904, Mr. Cobb, as Mammy called her husband, lost his right arm in a corn shredder on his farm. Between 1904 and 1906 his first wife died during a miscarriage; his older daughter died from appendicitis, and his younger daughter passed away after struggli[ng] with severe allergies.

He refused to give up on life. He remarried and h[ad] four daughters. During the Great Depression he lo[st] farms in Louisiana and Tennessee because cotton pric[es] plummeted from forty-five cents to five cents a poun[d]. Yet he told his family, "I slept as well that night as I ev[er] slept." He never complained about his multiple losses b[ut] continued to be one of the most generous and we[ll] beloved men in the county up until his death at a[ge] eighty-two. The legacy of his faith in God, h[is] indomitable spirit, and his refusal to bend to bitterne[ss] will endure in our family for many generations.

JOURNAL THOUGHTS

_____

_____

_____

_____

_____

_____

WEEK 16

Show me, O Lord, my life's end and the number of my days;
let me know how fleeting is my life. You have made my days a mere handbreadth;
the span of my years is as nothing before you. Each man's life is but a breath . . .
You rebuke and discipline men for their sin; you consume their wealth like a moth—
each man is but a breath.—Psalm 39:4–5, 11

Three times I've visited butterfly exhibits where the visitor is free to stroll through flowered paths as myriad colors of butterflies dance among the blossoms. It is magical to watch these quicksilver pixies that dust you with their fairy powders should they touch you in their passing.

We know scientifically that on average butterflies survive in terms of weeks, not years. Perhaps in God's time frame we are but butterflies. We know in our hearts that we have but a brief moment. Perhaps if we, too, tried to reflect beauty in our acts as we dance and glide through our days, we would rub off on others in our passing.

JOURNAL THOUGHTS

_____

_____

_____

_____

_____

_____

_____

_____

_____

_____

WEEK 17

Many, O Lord my God, are the wonders you have done.
The things you planned for us no one can recount to you;
were I to speak and tell of them, they would be too many to declare.—Psalm 40:5

In hiking a trail at Glacier National Park for the first time, I rounded a rock outcropping and nearly dropped to the ground as I was hit by sights, sounds, and smells so unexpectedly magnificent that they left me breathless. Curtains of white and gray clouds draped the shining blue sky and complemented the streaks of snow still hiding on the hillside from the pale, early summer sun.

A perfectly placed waterfall thundered off the mountain in the distance, yet I heard the cry of a red-tailed hawk soaring nearby. The fresh aroma of pine and spruce perfumed the air with the fragrance of everlasting green. Every sense was engaged. It was almost too much to absorb. Spontaneously, I began to sing that stirring Christian hymn, in my flat, off-key, but highly enthusiastic voice, "O Lord, my God, when I in awesome wonder, consider all the worlds Thy hands have made. . . . Then sings my soul, my Savior God to Thee; how great Thou art!"

How many times have we missed equal miraculous scenes designed by the Creator to refre and fill us because they are not so spectacular? Ho much do we fail to see the extraordinary in the ordina trails we travel at home? Look at your pet cat or do African violets, daffodils, blue jays, anything you s quite often. How would you describe it to someone wl is blind: the subtle colors, the textures, the personali the habits, everything that comes together to make it unique creation?

This one thing you've looked at is a miniscu fraction of God's creativity, in one tiny place on a spe of an insignificant planet, in one of millions of galaxi Our God, the Creator of uncountable worlds, does not neatly in the Sunday-size box we attempt to keep him How great Thou art!

JOURNAL THOUGHTS

_____

_____

_____

_____

_____

WEEK 18

As the deer pants for streams of water, so my soul pants for you,
O God. My soul thirsts for God, for the living God.
When can I go and meet with God?—Psalm 42:1–2

On my first medical-dental mission trip to Honduras, I worked as the group's photographer. During the ?t, twelve-hour workdays, I quickly realized how much I ?e water for granted. I've always lived in parts of our ?untry with high rainfall. I soak in the tub at least one ?ht a week. As an occasional runner, I normally drink a ? of water. Although I had traveled in third world ?untries before, this was my first time to live under the ?me conditions as the indigenous poor.

Whenever I needed to fill my water bottle in that little ?lage in Honduras, I had to use the water our team had ?nsported there in big metal drums and only that supply. ? bathe at night, we each got one bucketful of cold water. ?e second year I went, the area had withstood a drought ?r several months. A Christian couple in that village graciously shared their meager water supply so that our cooks could clean their pots and pans. They offered their most valuable possession because they were grateful we had brought ministers to preach and doctors to treat the people of their community. They traded well water for living water.

God is more necessary to us than drinking water, yet we trudge along the path ignoring our soul's thirst to our peril. We are so self-reliant. We think that we can do life all by ourselves, thank you very much. And we frantically run without regard to our spiritual health until our soul is parched and we finally collapse. When we truly seek, we discover that God was there all along with enough water to keep us going. We were just too focused on conquering the trail alone to notice.

JOURNAL THOUGHTS

_____

_____

_____

_____

_____

_____

_____

_____

WEEK 19

Send forth your light and your truth, let them guide me;
let them bring me to your holy mountain, to the place where you dwell.
Then will I go to the altar of God, to God my joy and my delight.
I will praise you with the harp, O God, my God.—Psalm 43:3–4

It is easy to understand the sacredness of mountains. They rise so far above us and point jagged fingers to heaven. Lightning dances around their heads. Their immovable solidity gives a sense of security. There is an otherworldliness about them, a mystery which piques our curiosity.

They remind us that at the end of the flood, Noah's ark nestled on the mountains of Ararat and humankind had a second chance at life. Moses met God on Mt. Sinai to receive the Ten Commandments and to give the Israelites a second chance to obedient.

While Jesus prayed on a mountaintop, Moses a Elijah appeared and talked with him, giving the th disciples with him another chance to believe in divinity. And, on a mountain in Galilee, Jesus met wi his eleven apostles for the last time to give them a chan to follow him by example and to teach God's ways others. Mountains invite us to come on foot or in o minds and give us another chance to meet God there, to

JOURNAL THOUGHTS

_____

_____

_____

_____

_____

_____

_____

_____

WEEK 20

God is our refuge and strength, an ever present help in trouble.
Therefore, we will not fear, though the earth give way and the mountains fall
into the heart of the sea, though its waters roar and foam
and the mountains quake with their surging.—Psalm 46:1–3

My husband and I were snorkeling near the harbor in Grand Cayman on an overcast, windy day. The water was whitecapping and kept splashing into my snorkel. I'm not much of a swimmer and have an inordinate fear of the ocean. The water was rougher than I could handle, and I really panicked. I was crying and gasping for air. If I had been alone, I don't know what would have happened. I grabbed my husband's flipper in front of me, and he immediately saw that I was in trouble. He quickly helped me get out of the deep and back to the rocky shore, calming me with his words as he led me to safety.

In much the same way, God always hears our cries for help and is close enough to reach out and pull us back to safety. When our personal world is falling apart and there is chaos everywhere we turn, his words can take away our fears if we give them up to him.

JOURNAL THOUGHTS

_____

_____

_____

_____

_____

_____

_____

_____

_____

WEEK 21

The Mighty One, God, the Lord, speaks and summons the earth
from the rising of the sun to the place where it sets. . . .
And the heavens proclaim his righteousness,
for God himself is judge.—Psalm 50:1, 6

John Keats wrote in his poem, "Ode on a Grecian Urn": "'Beauty is truth, truth beauty,'—that is all ye know on earth, and all ye need to know." At no time does this sentiment strike me as more accurate than at the sight of an irrefutably unique sunset. Something resonates in the core of my soul, and I can hear the echo of the deep voice of my childhood minister, Dr. Fred Kendall, reading from Genesis 1, verse 4: "And God saw the light, that it was good. . ." (KJV).

Sunsets are exclamation points at the end of a that can retrieve an otherwise commonplace date the calendar from obscurity and emblazon it forever your mind's eye as a day of unparalleled beauty. Th generate *oohs* and *aahs* as much or more than anythi in nature, except, perhaps, a newborn baby. They God's signatures on a twenty-four hour work of art.

JOURNAL THOUGHTS

_____

_____

_____

_____

_____

_____

_____

_____

WEEK 22

My heart is in anguish within me; the terrors of death assail me.
Fear and trembling have beset me; horror has overwhelmed me.
I said, "Oh, that I had the wings of a dove! I would fly away
and be at rest . . ."—Psalm 55:4–7

s the twentieth century careened to a close, the spectre of racial cleansing reared again in Europe, nding historians back to World War II for grim alogies. On a recent trip to Prague, that history took flesh and blood as we silently read through some of the hty thousand names listed on the walls of Pinkas nagogue. This was the majority of the Czechoslovakian vish population. Their names, dates of birth, and dates death were listed, encircling the walls. I found Oda ller, a forty-five year old whose death fell on my thday—a connection.

At the Spanish synagogue, we saw the artwork of the children who had been in Terezin and the programs for the plays and concerts they performed. This was the showplace concentration camp the Nazis used to placate the Red Cross. Later, these little ones were sent to their deaths in the concentration camps in the east. How like little birds they were: so bright and colorful. How they must have yearned to fly back to their parents' arms, to fly away from the confusion, hunger, and pain. Yet even in the midst of that despair, they created beauty and left a legacy of hope that survives today.

JOURNAL THOUGHTS

_____

_____

_____

_____

_____

_____

_____

_____

_____

_____

WEEK 23

I will praise you, O Lord, among the nations;
I will sing of you among the peoples. For great is your love,
reaching to the heavens; your faithfulness reaches to the skies.
Be exalted, O God, above the heavens;
let your glory be over all the earth.—Psalm 57:9–11

My older daughter and I stood for twenty minutes on a hot, dusty public bus carrying a laughing crowd of vagabond college students across the Greek island of Santorini one July afternoon. As we stepped off in Oia, we joined the streaming hordes of old, young, Greeks, and foreigners who poured through the narrow alleys of the whitewashed hamlet to get to the westernmost end of the island. There we perched en masse on stone walls, large boulders, and rocky ground amid the babble of many languages.

Wine, water, and colas poured into glasses. Laughter bubbled and eddied through the throng. Someone's radio began to quiet the crowds with the strains of classical music. The symphony lifted our hearts with its rightness for the moment. A hush of expectancy turned us all to the sea, and the sun began its glorious, dignified descent into the Aegean. And God was there.

JOURNAL THOUGHTS

_____

_____

_____

_____

_____

_____

_____

_____

WEEK 24

Find rest, O my soul, in God alone; my hope comes from him.
He alone is my rock and my salvation; he is my fortress, I will not be shaken.
My salvation and my honor depend on God; he is my mighty rock, my refuge.
Trust in him at all times, O people; pour out your hearts to him,
for God is our refuge.—Psalm 62:5–8

In 1906, President Theodore Roosevelt proclaimed Devil's Tower in northeast Wyoming America's first national monument. This 867-foot-high monolith rises out of relatively low rolling hills to astound the first-time visitor with its magnitude. One might imagine it serving for thousands of years as a landmark and probably a sacred site for generations, from the earliest inhabitants to the Arapaho, Cheyenne, and Sioux of the last two centuries. This was also the setting for a spaceship landing in the popular movie *Close Encounters of the Third Kind*.

Humankind instinctively sees significance in such special places. It is easy to imagine that something so much larger than ourselves, so still, so removed, could house the spirits of the other world. The familiar old hymn echoes the thought of these verses: "Rock of ages, cleft for me, let me hide myself in thee." If I climb the rock of ages and see the world from that perspective, it helps me realize there is a much larger view available than that which is down on my "I" level. Only God can save us from ourselves. We trust and confide our greatest hopes and failures in him so that God can help us cope and truly find rest.

JOURNAL THOUGHTS

_____

_____

_____

_____

_____

_____

_____

WEEK 25

O God, you are my God, earnestly I seek you;
my soul thirsts for you, in a dry and weary land where there is no water.
I have seen you in the sanctuary and beheld your power and your glory.
Because your love is better than life, my lips will glorify you.—Psalm 63:1–3

It is amazing how little rain falls in our deserts. The annual average is a mere 1.63 inches in Death Valley, California, compared to 460 inches annually on the island of Kauai, Hawaii. Just when everything living looks as though it has died and will blow away momentarily, the rains come all at once. They restore life that then bursts out of dried casings to stun you with its color and variety. It takes such a tiny bit of rain to encourage the flower within to spring forth.

Even in our desert days, the slightest drop of reassurance can refresh us and help us face another day. We can store up love much like the cactus stores water and can draw upon it for strength and sustenance in lean times. And, miraculously, we can share it with fellow travelers and it will get us all through the desert. Give someone a cup of water today.

JOURNAL THOUGHTS

_____

_____

_____

_____

_____

_____

_____

_____

WEEK 26

We all arrive at your doorstep sooner or later, loaded with guilt,
our sins are too much for us—but you get rid of them once and for all.
Blessed are the chosen! Blessed the guest at home in your place!
We expect our fill of good things in your house, your heavenly manse.
All your salvation wonders are on display in your trophy room.
Earth-Tamer, Ocean-Pourer, Mountain-Maker, Hill-Dresser, Muzzler of sea storm
and wave crash, of mobs in noisy riot—far and wide they'll come to a stop,
they'll stare in awe, in wonder. Dawn and dusk take turns calling,
"Come and worship."—Psalm 65:3–8 THE MESSAGE

Over and over we read in Scripture about the need for forgiveness. The only marital advice I remember other giving me was, "Don't ever go to bed mad." With few excruciating exceptions, I've tried to adhere to that. The mornings are ever so much better if you've cleared out the clouds of blame and frustration the night before.

We are told not to let the sun set on our anger. One full day without forgiving is too much, even when it's the need to forgive ourselves. Yet we continue to pile up day upon day of failures and sins on our shoulders so that we can't see where we're going. Finally we stumble into God. The Creator lifts that burden and says, "Look around this home I've given you. Let me help you. Enjoy what you have." Each new day is another beginning with its hope and assurance of more blessings.

No matter where on earth one lives (except perhaps in the polar regions), there is the chance twice a day to witness a sublime spectacle. The young morning sun shyly tiptoes in on pale pink slippers across the eastern sky. Later her older, gypsy cousin flounces out of sight in a flurry of orange, red, and gold, throwing on her black velvet shawl to signal the night. Both are cause for celebration for their beauty is universal and can be shared by all who take the time to look.

JOURNAL THOUGHTS

_____

_____

_____

_____

WEEK 27

Shout with joy to God, all the earth! Sing the glory of his name;
make his praise glorious! Say to God, "How awesome are your deeds!
So great is your power that your enemies cringe before you.
All the earth bows down to you, they sing praise to you,
they sing praise to your name."—Psalm 66:1–4

Years ago on the trip to Ireland with my parents, we were surprised to walk up on this immense waterfall at Powerscourt Estate outside of Dublin. The ground shook with the thunder of it. We have marveled at Niagara Falls in New York and its sister, Victoria Falls, in Zimbabwe. Seldom can you experience the full force of nature as directly as you can at the foot of a waterfall.

How insignificant it makes us feel! Even though I have toured Hoover Dam, I still don't understand how electricity is mechanically created through harnessi[ng] that raw power. I do feel something akin to an elect[ric] shock when the combination of the noise of the roari[ng] water and the vibration it sets off by the concussion [of] the rocks assaults my senses. This is the river's shout [of] joy to its maker and to all that have ears to hear.

We may be reluctant to do much shouti[ng] ourselves, but at a minimum a whispered prayer [of] praise is fitting.

JOURNAL THOUGHTS

_____

_____

_____

_____

_____

_____

_____

_____

WEEK 28

But you, O God, are my king from of old; you bring salvation upon the earth.
It was you who split open the sea by your power; you broke the heads
of the monster in the waters. . . . It was you who opened up springs and streams;
you dried up the ever flowing rivers. The day is yours, and yours also the night;
you established the sun and moon. It was you who set all the boundaries of the earth;
you made both summer and winter.—Psalm 74:12–13, 15–17

Flying with a bush pilot as we left the Mt. McKinley area on an Alaskan adventure, we were immediately transported from the lush green of summer grasses to a tranquil, frozen, mysterious ice world. Our tiny, puttering airplane was no more than an intrusive gnat to these massive shoulders of God. As we wheeled and darted down valleys filled with diamond-like cascades, I felt fragile and vulnerable.

There aren't enough superlatives in English or any other language to express the extent of God's characteristics because it is beyond our capacity to quantify what is truly a mystery. We look to the extremes of nature for analogies to help our pitifully finite minds grasp this magnificence.

We gawk at this alien sight of ancient snow and blue ice of glacier fields shimmering down the sides of the mountain range and we are silenced by their stark, cold grandeur. Yet, this God of snow and ice still takes time to care for us as well as for all living creatures. We don't understand why; we can only give thanks that it is true.

JOURNAL THOUGHTS

_____

_____

_____

_____

_____

_____

_____

WEEK 29

How lovely is your dwelling place, O Lord Almighty!
My soul yearns, even faints, for the courts of the Lord;
my heart and my flesh cry out for the living God.
Even the sparrow has found a home, and the swallow a nest for herself,
where she may have her young—a place near your altar, O Lord Almighty,
my king and my God. Blessed are these who dwell in your house;
they are ever praising you.—Psalm 84:1–4

The psalmist is talking about the beauty of Solomon's temple in Jerusalem five hundred to one thousand years before Christ. He is envious of the birds which have nested in the eaves so near to the Holy of Holies. God's temple is all of earth, a place of prodigious beauty where even the birds have been provided safe housing and sing their praises to the skies day and night.

We spend much of our lives looking for that safe place—a home, a retreat, a nest to bring us respite from cares and woes. If only we had the security of a certain amount of money. If only we had a high level competency in our work. If we were assured o relationships would last. Then we could really st worrying and take time to enjoy where we are.

I recently received the following e-mail passed alo by a close friend: "Good morning! This is God. I will handling all of your problems today. I will not need yo help. So, relax, and have a great day!" Our only su thing is that God loves us without reserve and always h the door open to his house for us to enter at will.

JOURNAL THOUGHTS

_____

_____

_____

_____

_____

_____

_____

_____

WEEK 30

Love and faithfulness meet together; righteousness and peace kiss each other.
Faithfulness springs forth from the earth, and righteousness looks down from heaven.
The Lord will indeed give what is good, and our land will yield its harvest.
Righteousness goes before him and prepares the way for his steps.—Psalm 85:10–13

ach spring, out of the seemingly dead, brown grassy remains of winter, arise extravagantly painted, ringly colorful tulips shouting, "We're back!" They stop in our tracks with their splendor and remind us that e can hang on through the dismal cold of winter and, in me, burst out anew, often stronger and better than ever.

When we reach the bottom of despair yet refuse to let go of the few shards of hope we still have in God, the ice in our hearts begins to melt and our snow blindness heals. We see again how God has led us through our trials. His faithfulness to us yields a harvest of spiritual revival of love and peace as extraordinary as that of tulips.

JOURNAL THOUGHTS

_____

_____

_____

_____

_____

_____

_____

_____

_____

_____

WEEK 31

You are forgiving and good, O Lord,
abounding in love to all who call you. Hear my prayer, O Lord;
listen to my cry for mercy. In the day of my trouble I will call to you,
for you will answer me. —Psalm 86:5–7

My best friend and I went to South Dakota to explore an area neither of us had ever visited. After marveling at the herd of bison still roaming in Custer State Park, we were lured by a dot on the map marked "Mammoth." There we found a site where thousands of years ago a precursor of the bison, the mastodon, ruled the plains. Some of them, along with other ancient animals, became entrapped in a sinkhole, where their remains lay hidden until a local contractor uncovered them as he cleared land for a municipal building.

At his insistence, the city stopped the development Today a museum stands over the pit and you can s many bones left in the exact places the animals die Their mistake in wandering into the slimy hole evident for all to view. But for the grace of God, t bones of many of my own earlier mistakes would be display for all to see. Instead, the God of second chanc gave me a foothold on solid ground and pulled me o of the mire so that I could move on. That hand is he out for you, too.

JOURNAL THOUGHTS

_____

_____

_____

_____

_____

_____

_____

_____

WEEK 32

Your throne was established long ago; you are from all eternity.
The seas have lifted up, O Lord, the seas have lifted up their voice;
the seas have lifted up their pounding waves.
Mightier than the thunder of the great waters, mightier than the breakers of the sea—
the Lord on high is mighty. Your statutes stand firm;
holiness adorns your house for endless days, O Lord.—Psalm 93:2–5

According to some biblical commentators, seas and storms were an often-used Hebrew symbol of chaos and trouble. To watch the constant surging and pounding of white surf on rocks and sand during turbulence gives one a taste of the potential for destruction that the ocean has. The wind tearing through your hair and the driving rain stinging your eyes as the roar of the waves heightens make you feel weak and helpless in the face of such force. Yet God can calm the storm and let peace return. In like manner, our Lord can bring order out of the chaos we make in our lives so we are not washed away and lost.

In the second trimester of two of our pregnancies, the waters of my womb broke prematurely and crashed our hope of new life to join our family. Two perfectly formed, miniature boys, flesh of our flesh, never got to see our smiles or feel our hugs. And I thought I would drown with the pain of loss. Gradually, through the love and prayer of family and friends, I became immensely grateful for the health of the three-year-old son we did have. I began to truly marvel at the everyday changes in him and how the world looked through his eyes. And I found peace.

JOURNAL THOUGHTS

_____

_____

_____

_____

_____

_____

WEEK 33

*Come, let us sing for joy to the Lord; let us shout aloud
to the Rock of our salvation. Let us come before him with thanksgiving
and extol him with music and song. For the Lord is the great God,
the great King above all gods. In his hand are the depths of the earth,
and the mountain peaks belong to him. The sea is his, for he made it,
and his hands formed the dry land. Come, let us bow down in worship,
let us kneel before the Lord our Maker; for he is our God
and we are the people of his pasture, the flock under his care.—Psalm 95:1–7*

One of my early memories of childhood play is after a long rain when the gutters in the street were full of water. I made boats out of small pieces of cardboard and folded up newspaper. I dammed up the flood with rocks, bricks, and sticks. I never controlled the flow for very long, and I ran alongside my fleet as it raced down to the street grate of the storm drain.

Whenever I see a lighthouse on a rocky coastline, I can't help but wonder what stories it would tell if it could talk. How many ships and small boats wou[ld] have run aground in fog or blinding rain but f[or] the faithful signal light which flashed through th[e] curtain of darkness, blinking the message, "Dange[r] Turn back! Run to safety!" I believe the sea as we[ll] as the rocks are God's, but I am grateful that h[e] cares enough about his people to give us a light i[n] the dark, his word, to help us chart our way throug[h] dangerous shoals.

JOURNAL THOUGHTS

_____

_____

_____

_____

_____

_____

_____

WEEK 34

For great is the Lord and most worthy of praise; he is to be feared above all gods.
For all the gods of the nations are idols, but the Lord made the heavens.
Splendor and majesty are before him; strength and glory are in his sanctuary. . . .
Let the heavens rejoice, let the earth be glad; let the sea resound,
and all that is in it; let the fields be jubilant, and everything in them.
Then all the trees of the forest will sing for joy; they will sing before the Lord,
for he comes, he comes to judge the earth. He will judge the world in righteousness
and the peoples in his truth.—Psalm 96:4–6;11–13

go to our lake house, an hour from our home, to watch and to hear the forest sing for joy. It sings a different song each season. In winter, the dead leaves and pine needles cushion the path. They muffle my steps as I try to glimpse a passing deer. I can imagine a low, mournful dirge playing in the bare branches of the oaks. In spring, a sprightly tune sung by wrens, finches, and warblers flitting among the white dogwood and wild pink azaleas makes me hurry along the trail.

Summer's woodsy symphony is lush with whippoorwill, bullfrogs, crickets, and the staccato beat of woodpeckers drilling massive tree limbs for insects. An autumn concert might consist of a prelude of burbling springs and sighing pines, followed by the crisp crackling of golden, red, and orange-bright leaves as foxes scamper through the forest floor. Each season has its unique song, but all sing for joy.

JOURNAL THOUGHTS

_____

_____

_____

_____

_____

_____

_____

WEEK 35

Let the sea resound, and everything in it, the world,
and all who live in it. Let the rivers clasp their hands,
let the mountains sing together for joy; let them sing before the Lord,
for he comes to judge the earth. He will judge the world in righteousness
and the peoples with equity.—Psalm 98:7–9

We have to almost make ourselves get away from home and work before we can relax and look about us to enjoy nature. We don't have it scheduled in our appointment book; it's not one of our production goals for the month. We seldom give ourselves permission to just be. Maybe it's our puritan work ethic, but most of us feel like we must always be consciously productive.

However, if we inadvertently get a taste of it, on vacation or a business trip, what good medicine it can be. Natural beauty can lighten our burdens and direct our thoughts to a Creator much bigger than ourselves. We breathe more deeply and slow our step to take it in. If you knew you had only a few months to live, would you make different choices about how you spend your time? Put life into whatever time you have left.

JOURNAL THOUGHTS

_____

_____

_____

_____

_____

_____

_____

_____

WEEK 36

Hear my prayer, O Lord, let my cry for help come to you.
Do not hide your face from me when I am in distress.
Turn your ear to me; when I call, answer me quickly.
For my days vanish like smoke; my bones burn like glowing embers.
My heart is blighted and withered like grass; I forget to eat my food.
Because of my loud groaning I am reduced to skin and bones.
I am like a desert owl, like an owl among the ruins.—Psalm 102:1–6

A mystery is solved. Unspeakable fears take root in a word. Stunned, the days ahead stretch into a short road leading to despair. Like the false mirage of water on a blistering highway in simmering summer heat, there's the anticipation of help from chemotherapy or radiation. Surely they can kill these lunatic cells which threaten the life of a child, a parent, friend or lover.

The hospital becomes a desert and flesh withers and dries out from treatments which are themselves a mini-death of cells, good and bad alike. Mothers and fathers break their hearts and offer them up in exchange for relief for meager skin barely covering fragile bones and the soul of their child. Each person is at last alone and cries out, like the desert owl, "Who, who, who is there?" God gently answers, "I am."

JOURNAL THOUGHTS

_____

_____

_____

_____

_____

_____

_____

_____

_____

WEEK 37

God is sheer mercy and grace; not easily angered,
he's rich in love. He doesn't endlessly nag and scold, nor hold grudges forever.
He doesn't treat us as our sins deserve, nor pay us back in full for our wrongs.
As high as heaven is over the earth, so strong is his love to those who fear him.
—Psalm 103:8–11 THE MESSAGE

As a parent, I hate to think of the accumulation of nagging and fussing I've done living with four children. I hope that won't be the first thing they think of in remembering me. As a new parent, I was afraid if I let any unacceptable behavior go unpunished, I would be spending my retirement years visiting my offspring in various prisons across the South. With each successive child, I lightened up a bit so that number four has it relatively easy according to his older brother and sisters.

God doesn't hold on to his anger and he doesn punish us for all the things we do wrong. For that I eternally grateful. I truly experience forgiveness when repent of wrongdoing and believe that God wants me let go of the guilt I feel. Every time I see a rainbow, am reminded what a wonderful gift it is: God's promis He is still with us after the rains of life and loves intensely. It takes the rain to shape the light and refra it to create the glorious rainbow. It takes the sorrows help us appreciate the beauty of ordinary normalcy.

JOURNAL THOUGHTS

_____

_____

_____

_____

_____

_____

_____

_____

WEEK 38

As a father has compassion on his children,
so the Lord has compassion on those who fear him.
For he knows how we are formed, he remembers that we are dust.
As for man, his days are like grass, he flourishes like a flower of the field;
the wind blows over it and it is gone, and its place remembers it no more.
But from everlasting to everlasting the Lord's love is with those who fear him,
and his righteousness with their children's children . . .—Psalm 103:13–17

We really owe a debt of thanks to Lady Bird Johnson, wife of former President Lyndon Johnson. She itiated the sowing of wildflower seeds along the medians d public highways in Texas in the seventies. Her success ere has generated many followers who have decorated state ads from coast to coast with ribbons of scarlet, purple, ue, and yellow blooms. Although the season is short, the lendid surprise of this burst of beauty relieves the tedium interstate driving and is a gift to weary travelers.

Mrs. Johnson certainly gave her energy and time and oney for many other good causes, but I wonder if anything else has brought as much pleasure to as many people for almost thirty years as her flower planting has. Beauty resonates in each of us regardless of our intelligence, education, age, sex, race, or culture. It lifts our spirits, and gives us hope and encouragement that ideals do exist.

She was one person with a simple notion of making a roadside pretty for every passerby. What would happen if each of us added beauty to our own roadside by cleaning up a neighborhood, helping paint murals on blighted walls, or by showing children the joy of planting and growing flowers with God?

JOURNAL THOUGHTS

_____

_____

_____

_____

_____

_____

_____

_____

WEEK 39

Sunrise breaks through the darkness for good people—
God's grace and mercy and justice! The good person is generous and lends lavishly,
no stumbling around for this one, but a sterling and solid and lasting reputation.
Unfazed by rumor and gossip, heart ready, trusting in God, spirit firm, unperturbed,
ever blessed, relaxed among enemies, they lavish gifts on the poor—a generosity
that goes on, and on, and on. An honored life! A beautiful life!
—Psalm 112:4–9 THE MESSAGE

The optimist is searching the darkness for those first rays of light to signal the emergence of the sun again. I immediately thought of my husband when I read this passage. He is bone-deep good, one of the most self-effacing and quietly generous persons I know. He puts others first and doesn't expect to be noticed for it.

He finds good even in those people others have given up on. I have observed his stubborn loyalty as he gives a second or third chance to individuals one would, at be call misfits. And they usually rise to his expectation surprising us cynics. Of course, not everyone measures u but when there is disappointment, he takes bad news hea on and shoulders the responsibilities that go with it wi grace and without blaming others. He clearly reflects f faith in and love of God day by day with his compassion f people around him. He is God's great gift to our family.

JOURNAL THOUGHTS

_____

_____

_____

_____

_____

_____

_____

WEEK 40

This is the day the Lord has made,
let us rejoice and be glad in it.
O Lord, save us; O Lord, grant us success.
—*Psalm 118:24–25*

If we awakened tomorrow morning and said this verse before we crawled out of bed and really took it to heart, how different might that day be? "This is another chance to get it right, God. I thank you for letting me be here. Help me be the best I can be." Isn't that what real success is—making our gifts, talents, and circumstances and using those to become the loving individual God intended us to be?

We spend too much of our time reliving our past: agonizing over our failures, imagined and real, embroidering on slights done to us, or nostalgically savoring especially delicious days that have slipped away. Another big chunk of time is spent planning tomorrow, or next week, or next month. Where will we be? What will we be doing? Few of us are really good at living now, in this moment. This is the day we have. When it passes through the setting sun, it will not return. Tomorrow might not arrive. We cannot change yesterday. Savor today. Taste it with gratitude.

JOURNAL THOUGHTS

_____

_____

_____

_____

_____

_____

_____

_____

WEEK 41

Your decrees are my song in the place of my exile.
By night I remember your name, O God. I will keep your law.
This is my blessing: that I have observed your precepts.
—Psalm 119:54–56 PSALMS ANEW

A number of prisoners of war share stories of maintaining their sanity while in solitary confinement without paper or pen by focusing on Bible verses and hymns memorized as children. Their endurance of intense physical and mental deprivation was eased by God's presence through words that took on new meaning and were made real by their relevance. Their dark night of the soul was made tolerable through the grace of memory, and they fervently thanked God for all the good things of life they could recount in their minds.

What comfort there was as a child to pray, "Now I lay me down to sleep. I pray the Lord my soul to keep. If I should die before I wake, I pray the Lord my soul to take."

I'm grateful my parents put my feet on the path of prayer by habitually sitting with me at bedtime, after telling me a story, to hear my prayers. They made it part of our nightly ritual, and I knew it was important because they took time to do it.

So it seems natural to me to remember God before sleep. When I veer off track because I'm tired or preoccupied and fail to do so, then the next day I know I've missed a blessing. I remind myself of the POW experiences and rejoice that I have free access to Scripture and teachings. If I had to rely on memory, how long would it take me to exhaust my supply of verses and hymns? Today I will learn this verse.

JOURNAL THOUGHTS

_____

_____

_____

_____

_____

_____

_____

WEEK 42

I lift up my eyes to the hills—where does my help come from?
My help comes from the Lord, the Maker of heaven and earth. . . .
The Lord watches over you—the Lord is your shade at your right hand.
The sun will not harm you by day, nor the moon by night.
The Lord will keep you from all harm—he will watch over your life;
the Lord will watch over your coming and going
both now and forevermore.—Psalm 121:1–2; 5–8

God does indeed watch over our lives. I have an aunt who is perhaps the saintliest person I know. She had a disastrous early marriage that ended in divorce, leaving her with two babies. Her beautiful little girl contracted an undiagnosed, catastrophic disease as a toddler and never recovered. She was so mentally and physically damaged that my aunt fed, diapered, and bathed her every day of her life, which stretched over forty years. She also had four other children she loved and cared for, and she still managed to maintain a great sense of humor.

I always looked forward to visiting my cousins in the summer because my aunt would take us on exciting expeditions: to see a haunted house, have a sunrise breakfast on the river, and cook out on an old cast-iron stove. And how we would laugh! No one would know to look at her the heartache she had coped with.

Each day she gets up at 5:00 A.M. and reads her Bible and studies and prays for an hour or more. She has countless notebooks full of quotations she has pulled from the hundreds of inspirational books and articles she has read each year. Weekly, she bakes many loaves of bread with which to feed the sick, the newcomers, and the shut-ins. Her discipline, faithfulness, and trust in God has influenced hundreds. She knows where her help comes from.

JOURNAL THOUGHTS

_____

_____

_____

_____

_____

WEEK 43

The Mount Zion referenced in this verse still endures today. It was the mountain where Solomon's temple was built and where the last temple was destroyed in A.D. 70 by the Roman general Titus. Today it is the site of the Moslem mosque called the Dome of the Rock, built over the sacred rock from where it is believed Mohammed left earth and ascended to heaven. Millions of people over many centuries—Christians, Jews, and Moslems—have taken comfort from the fact of its endurance.

Its namesake, Zion National Park in Utah encompasses a natural beauty that also evokes memories of ancient temples. Geologists tell us that the oldest deposits in that park hold marine fossils 245 million years old. Geology can be seen as a calendar to remind us that God's faithfulness to his creatures has lasted for eons and will be with us forever.

JOURNAL THOUGHTS

_____

_____

_____

_____

_____

_____

_____

_____

WEEK 44

Don't you see that children are God's best gift?
The fruit of the womb his generous legacy? Like a warrior's fistful of arrows
are the children of a vigorous youth. Oh, how blessed are you parents,
with your quivers full of children!—Psalm 127:3–5 THE MESSAGE

After my first son was born, following a textbook-perfect, easy pregnancy, I had two second-trimester miscarriages and feared we would not be able to have any more children. We had always planned on a large family, and I was devastated. How sweet was the birth of our daughter after my doctor found a medical solution to my problem. We were then able to successfully have two more babies, a daughter and a son. My greatest contribution to life has been the birthing of my four children who have brought us great joy.

But I worry about the other children I see who have come into homes where they were not anxiously awaited and loved. My heart aches for those I see with such promising possibilities and no one to encourage them. I am frustrated and angry with governments, local and national, which continually refuse to put the welfare of all our children as a priority of policy. How can we turn our backs on the need to feed, house, teach, protect, and love every child born in this nation? They are part of our quiver, too.

JOURNAL THOUGHTS

_____

_____

_____

_____

_____

_____

_____

_____

_____

WEEK 45

Out of the depths I cry to you, O God. God, hear my voice!
Let your ears be attentive to my cry for mercy. If you, O God, mark our guilt,
who can stand? But with you is forgiveness; and for this we revere you. . . .
For with you is faithful love and plentiful redemption.
—Psalm 130:1–4; 7 PSALMS ANEW

The few times we went to the panhandle of Florida when I was a child were magical to me. No sand is as white and sugar-soft as it was on those beaches. My little sister and I ran up and down the beach, leaving munchkin prints behind. The bubbling white surf quickly lapped them up, erasing our steps as though we had never been there. God moves along behind us in the same way, daily washing away our failures with grace and giving us fresh sand to walk on.

We carry on our backs the mistakes and sins of o[ur] past. Sometimes we don't seem to want to let go and dr[op] these burdens. We become comfortable dragging them around. Yet God is all about forgiveness—about wipi[ng] the sand clean. The Bible is replete with verses remindi[ng] us that there is nothing we can do that cannot [be] forgiven. If God can forgive us all the things we have do[ne] or failed to do, both trivial and terrible, why can we n[ot] forgive ourselves?

JOURNAL THOUGHTS

WEEK 46

My heart is not proud, O Lord, my eyes are not haughty.
I do not concern myself with great matters or things too wonderful for me.
But I have stilled and quieted my soul; like a weaned child with its mother,
like a weaned child is my soul within me.—Psalm 131:1–2

The wonder of having babies or grandchildren can slow our breakneck speed and serve as a scenic overlook on life's highway. We take note of the miracle of molecules that mirrors our smile or our eyes. We slow down momentarily to admire a new beginning and recall some of our own early sensations at the discovery of life.

On each of my medical-dental mission trips to Honduras I saw babies nursing while their mothers were in line to see the doctor or dentist or to get eyeglasses. They might have been whimpering or crying to get their mother's attention, but once they were satisfied with their milky meal they drifted off to sleep despite the hubbub of the milling crowds.

How rarely do we see such contentment in ourselves or in each other. We go from plan A to plan B. Seldom do we rest on our laurels, for there are always more races to run, more money to make, more titles to acquire, more hearts to break, more trophies to win, more stuff to own. It seems it takes either living a very long time, or suddenly learning we have very little time left to live, before we recognize the real beauty and value of each hour, each day as unique and irreplaceable. How long has it been since you felt real peace?

JOURNAL THOUGHTS

_____

_____

_____

_____

_____

_____

_____

_____

_____

WEEK 47

Where can I go from your spirit? Where can I flee from your presence?
If I go up to the heavens, you are there;
if I make my bed in the depths, you are there.
If I rise on the wings of the dawn, if I settle on the far side of the sea,
even there your hand will guide me, your right hand will hold me fast.
—Psalm 139:7–10

As an adult I recognize that God is inexplicably everywhere at the same time, but the child in me still imagines the Deity looking down from a heavenly kingdom. That's one reason I take such delight in flying, because I secretly feel Godlike seeing the world from that vantage point.

Being open to the people whose paths intersect ours, being aware of opportunities that come our way, and being conscious that there may be lessons to learn through these experiences helps keep us attuned to God. A few years ago I read an unattributed quote which has become a touchstone: "Coincidence is God's way of remaining anonymous."

When I ignore God or forget his presence for a while, something tugs at me, and I am reminded that no matter where I go, God's hand is there. It may be music unexpectedly touching my soul. It may be the innocent laugh of a child. It may be on the other side of the world as I watch the sun shake out rosy silk clouds to begin the day. And it may be the words from a chance encounter that give me exactly what I need at that moment, and I feel God's presence.

JOURNAL THOUGHTS

_____

_____

_____

_____

_____

_____

_____

WEEK 48

For you created my inmost being;
you knit me together in my mother's womb.
I praise you because I am fearfully and wonderfully made;
your works are wonderful, I know that full well.
My frame was not hidden from you when I was made in the secret place.
When I was woven together in the depths of the earth,
your eyes saw my unformed body.
All the days ordained for me were written in your book
before one of them came to be.—Psalm 139:13–16

count it an unparalleled privilege to have borne children. With the birth of each of my four I was so in awe of the process and so humbled to be able to participate in it with the Creator that I can still recall the rush of emotions. Because I was older when I carried our fourth child, I had a sonogram. How incredible it was to see a picture of my baby inside me! With my own eyes I could see him months before he came. I watched him move and heard his heartbeat. Not until he was actually born, though, did I feel completely secure about his health.

When that new life is first placed in your arms and you have counted all the perfectly formed fingers and toes, an overwhelming sense of joy and gratitude pours from you. Your heart almost bursts with love. You imagine a perfect future for your little one. Projecting ahead you see good health, ambition, popularity, intelligence . . . no bad things to mar your unqualified love. God sees beyond that birthing room to the disappointments, the pains, and the failures ahead and still loves that little one with full knowledge of the peaks and valleys. That God knows us for who we really are and cherishes us . . . that is the good news of the gospel.

JOURNAL THOUGHTS

_____

_____

_____

_____

_____

WEEK 49

If you wake me each morning with the sound of your loving voice,
I'll go to sleep each night trusting in you. Point out the road I must travel;
I'm all ears, all eyes before you. Save me from my enemies,
God—you're my only hope! Teach me how to live to please you,
because you're my God. Lead me by your blessed Spirit
into cleared and level pastureland.—Psalm 143:8–10 THE MESSAGE

I believe that God speaks to us with many voices. On spring mornings I hear him in the liquid trill of a pair of courageous Carolina wrens who for several years have nested in a wreath of artificial forsythia and roses on our front porch. I had originally hung it on our front door but moved it to the wall when I discovered these busy little neighbors building in it. I can peer out the side windows to see them flit back and forth.

We've startled each other on a number of occasions. The nesting bird flies to a nearby limb to fuss at me. At odd times as I work in my study, I hear them serenading, and stop and marvel that after fourteen years wrens are still her When we were building our house, I came over or afternoon and stood on the slab that would be our mast bedroom. Suddenly two baby wrens scurried across th concrete, with an adult close behind them. I saw that as blessing on our home because their songs are so uplifting Such a powerful, clear bit of music from a handful of brow feathers, sending echoes of beauty out into the world. Liste for God's voice this week in the birds around you.

JOURNAL THOUGHTS

_____

_____

_____

_____

_____

_____

WEEK 50

Make our sons in their prime like sturdy oak trees,
our daughters as shapely and bright as fields of wildflowers.
Fill our barns with great harvest, fill our fields with huge flocks;
Protect us from invasion and exile—eliminate the crime in our streets.
—*Psalm 144:12–15* THE MESSAGE

What a contemporary prayer this is: petitions for health, food, protection, and peace. These are basics that everyone desires. We are blessed to live in a country where these conditions are generally good for most citizens, but not for all. Part of our responsibility as children of God is to use our talents and material possessions to be our brother's (and sister's) keeper. When we take stock of what we have, how do we share it so that this prayer can be answered for others?

Do we teach our children at an early age to appreciate what they have? To give time and energy to volunteering in their school, church, or community for some good cause? Do we invest ourselves by example in projects that will live on in the lives of generations to come? Do we pay attention to electing officials of character to lead our cities, school boards, state and national governments? We are partners with God in creating a better world for our grandchildren to enjoy. May they have reason to thank us for our stewardship.

JOURNAL THOUGHTS

_____

_____

_____

_____

_____

_____

_____

_____

_____

WEEK 51

Sing to God with thanksgiving; sing praise with the harp to our God,
who covers the heavens with clouds, who provides rain for the earth,
and who makes grass grow on the mountains, who gives food to the cattle,
and to the young ravens when they call. God does not delight
in the strength of the steed, nor is God pleased with the fleetness of humans.
God is pleased with those who have reverence, with those who hope in faithful love.
—*Psalm 147:7–11 PSALMS ANEW*

At our table we say a blessing before our meals, but it is often perfunctory, thrown up quickly so the food won't get cold. "Bless this food to the nourishment of our bodies, and us to Thy service," or, "God is great, God is good, and we thank him for our food." What bounty God has provided for us— the richness of soils, the diversity of seeds, and the cycles of weather. We do take so much for granted in a culture that is several steps removed from digging in the dirt and personally harvesting its sustenance.

There was a summer project in our city where children and older adults had the opportunity to plant small garden plots on some vacant land in a blighted urban area. It was the first time the young people had ever had the experienc of watching something grow that they had planted. For th retirees, it brought back memories of growing up in th hardscrabble, rural south where poke sallet, turnip green and fatback were staples. There was a lesson in the enthusiasm and excitement at picking their own tomatoe beans, and squash. They were truly thankful.

Because God is the origin of all that we have and se the one thing we can do to show our thankfulness is t exercise our free will and choose to serve God out of lov and appreciation. When we demonstrate our faith an trust by our obedience to God's word, we are living ou our love. That is our gift in return.

JOURNAL THOUGHTS

_____

_____

_____

_____

_____

_____

WEEK 52

Praise God from earth, you sea dragons, you fathomless ocean deeps;
Fire and hail, snow and ice, hurricanes obeying his orders;
Mountains and all hills, apple orchards and cedar forest;
Wild beasts and herds of cattle, snakes, and birds in flight;
Earth's kings and all races, leaders and important people,
robust men and women in their prime, yes, graybeards and little children.
Let them praise the name of God—it's the only Name worth praising.
His radiance exceeds anything in earth and sky;
he's built a monument—his very own people!
Praise from all who love God!—Psalm 148:7–13 THE MESSAGE

f we began at dawn and prayed nonstop until sunset every day, we could not begin to praise the Creator sufficiently for all the blessings given to us. I love to go o the beach and have never stayed long enough to tire of . I find that the rhythm of the tides and the constancy f the surf are so soothing that they subtly realign the utlines of my days and nights and slow my pulse.

The tide is God's heartbeat. I am quieted, and I am omforted as a little girl in her mother's arms is lulled to rest by a measured heart. Walking along the shore and looking at the vast night sky, I make the time to praise and thank God. Sunrises and sunsets over water seem more dramatic, much grander than what I see at home. They lure me with their vibrant hues and breathtaking cloud compositions. May we never be immune to the jolt of awe that comes from natural beauty, nor forgetful of praising the Lord of Creation for it.

JOURNAL THOUGHTS

_____

_____

_____

_____

_____

JOURNAL THOUGHTS

_____

_____

_____

_____

_____

_____

_____

_____

_____

_____

_____

_____

_____

_____

_____

_____

_____

JOURNAL THOUGHTS

JOURNAL THOUGHTS

JOURNAL THOUGHTS

JOURNAL THOUGHTS

JOURNAL THOUGHTS

JOURNAL THOUGHTS

JOURNAL THOUGHTS

JOURNAL THOUGHTS

JOURNAL THOUGHTS

JOURNAL THOUGHTS

ABOUT THE PHOTOGRAPHS

ABOUT THE AUTHOR

Rebecca Webb Wilson is an avid traveler and amateur nature photographer. After a brief stint as a realtor, she attended law school at the University of Memphis and served several years as an Assistant United States Attorney. Following that career and after the birth of her fourth child, she became involved with the Memphis Zoological Society in its efforts to remodel and revitalize its facility. In 1988 she founded a youth leadership program in Memphis called Bridge Builders, which currently has participants in all public, private, and parochial schools. A graduate of Vanderbilt University, she serves as a member of its Board of Trust.

Rebecca Wilson is a deacon at Second Baptist Church in Memphis, Tennessee. She has authored meditations for devotional guides and Sunday school material for youth.

Ms. Wilson and her husband, Spence L. Wilson, have two sons and two daughters.